D1123917

# THE CIVIL WAR

# DIVIDED IN TWO

## The Road to Civil War, 1861

James R. Arnold and Roberta Wiener

LERNER PUBLICATIONS COMPANY • MINNEAPOLIS

**First American edition published in 2002
by Lerner Publications Company**

The Civil War series is created and produced by Graham Beehag Books,
in cooperation with Lerner Publications Company, a division of
Lerner Publishing Group.

Lerner Publications Company
A division of Lerner Publishing Group
241 First Avenue North
Minneapolis, Minnesota 55401 U.S.A.

Website address: www.lernerbooks.com

**Library of Congress Cataloging-in-Publication Data**

Arnold, James R.
  Divided in two : the road to civil war, 1861 / by James R. Arnold and
  Roberta Wiener.
    p. cm. – (The Civil War)
Includes bibliographical references and index.
  ISBN 0-8225-2312-4 (lib. bdg. : alk. paper)
  1. United States–History–Civil War, 1861–1865–Causes–
Juvenile literature.  2. United States—History—
Civil War, 1861–1865—Juvenile literature. [1. United States—
History—Civil War, 1861–1865—Causes.  2. United States—History—
Civil War,  1861–1865.]  I.  Wiener, Roberta,
1952–  II. Title.  III. Civil War (Minneapolis, Minn.)
E468.9 .A7   2002
973.7'11–dc21                                    00-011639


Printed in Singapore
Bound in the United States of America
1 2 3 4 5 6 – OS – 07 06 05 04 03 02

The authors wish to extend their special thanks to Joan E. Arnold of
Worcester, Massachusetts, who contributed the essay "The Abolitionists."

The authors are also grateful to Kate Kjorlien, whose excellent editing of
the manuscript has made this book such a pleasure to read.

*Front cover picture: Bombardment of Fort Sumter, 1861*

*Back cover picture: A cartoon shows Lincoln and Douglas
fighting in the presidential election of 1860.*

# Contents

# WORDS YOU NEED TO KNOW

**abolitionist:** a person who wanted to abolish, or end, slavery in the United States

**arsenal:** a building where weapons and ammunition are stored

**artillery:** a group of cannons and other large guns used by armies to fire at enemy soldiers

**civil war:** a war between two groups who are citizens of the same country

**compromise:** an agreement in which each side gives up some of the things it wants

**Confederacy:** another name for the Confederate States of America, the states that left the United States to form their own nation

**faction:** a group of people that forms within a larger group because it disagrees with many people in the larger group

**federal:** having to do with the central government of the United States

**free soil:** a state or territory where slavery was forbidden

**inauguration:** the ceremony marking the beginning of a new president's time in office

**neutral:** not taking a side

**plantation:** a very large farm, with hundreds of acres, in the Southern United States. A plantation usually grew a single crop and had slaves to do the work. The owner of a plantation was called a planter.

**rebels:** the nickname used by Northerners to refer to the citizens of the Southern states, who were in rebellion against the United States

**secession:** the action of a state seceding from, or withdrawing from, the United States

**states' rights:** the Southern belief that individual states had a wide range of rights, including the right to decide about slavery and the right to leave the United States

**territory:** an area of land in the United States that is not part of a state

**Union:** the Northern states that remained part of the United States during the Civil War

**Yankees:** the Southern nickname for the citizens of the Northern states

# One Nation, Two Sides

In 1776 soldiers from thirteen different states marched side by side to fight the Revolutionary War against Great Britain. They battled for independence with the rallying cry "United we stand, divided we fall." They faced danger, cold, and hunger for a cause they all shared. They thought of themselves not as Northerners or Southerners, but as Americans. They called their new nation the United States of America.

Yet in 1861, citizens of the United States were at war again. This time they fought one another in a terrible civil war between the Northern states and the Southern states. The soldiers were the grandchildren of the people who had fought and suffered to win the Revolutionary War. How could Americans unite in 1776 but then fight each other from 1861 to 1865?

The words *united states* mean "a union of states." In 1860 leaders of some Southern states believed that each state should be free to make its own choices. They believed that each state could choose whether or not to be part of the United States. Leaders of some Northern states disagreed. They believed that all the states should stay united. They worried that if a state could leave the United States whenever people disagreed, the nation their ancestors had fought to create would fall apart. It nearly did. The North and the South disagreed strongly with each other. This led to the Civil War—the bloodiest war in American history.

# CHAPTER ONE

# Taking Two Paths

In the years leading to the Civil War, the North and South had been growing apart. Northerners and Southerners had very different ways of life.

In the Southern states, wealthy white men spent their riches on land. They bought the best land, near the seacoast and along the rivers, and created huge farms called plantations. On the plantations, the owners grew tobacco, cotton, rice, and indigo. The plantation owners called themselves planters. But they were not the ones who planted the crops.

Growing tobacco, cotton, rice, and indigo was a hard job and required many workers. The planters hired poor white people and purchased slaves to do the labor. The slaves were black people whose ancestors had been captured in Africa and brought to America in crowded ships. The slaves had no rights in America. Their white owners were their masters. There was no question about how things worked. The white master was in charge, and the black slave had to obey. Some masters treated their slaves well, but others did not.

Some planters became very rich. They built great houses called mansions. The richest plantation owners were often political leaders in the South. They governed cities and states and sent their sons to college in England or to

*A family of slaves in front of their cabin. By the 1860s, the population of the United States included four million slaves.*

7

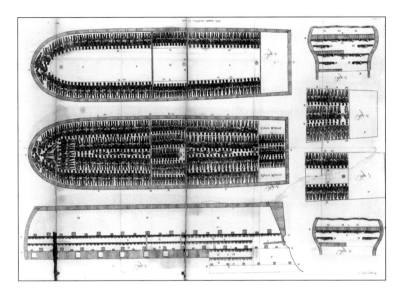

*Over time slave traders brought thousands of Africans across the Atlantic Ocean to America. The captives were chained and packed tightly into ships, left, so that the slave traders would have more people to sell at the end of the voyage. Many captives died on the ships from disease, cold, and starvation.*

fine schools in the North. Many of these sons became lawyers and political leaders too. They were the most powerful men in the South.

Southerners thought that their way of life was just right for them. They believed that slavery was "a blessing to the slave, and a blessing to the master." They felt that people with darker skin were not really human beings. So they thought that it was all right to own black slaves.

Life in the North was quite different. Northern farms were not as big as Southern plantations. The weather was colder, so Northerners did not grow the same kinds of crops.

In 1807 the United States made it illegal to import (bring in) slaves from Africa. Yet in 1860, the U.S. Navy captured an American ship called the Wildfire. It held more than five hundred African slaves, right, all of them naked and starving.

A cotton plantation on the Mississippi River, below. Slaves did the hardest physical work, such as digging ditches and harvesting cotton.

Instead, they raised corn, wheat, vegetables, and hay for livestock. Slavery was legal in the North, but most farmers did not own slaves. Instead, family members and hired workers did the farmwork. Northern farmers lived comfortably without owning slaves.

Some Northerners moved to towns and cities, where they worked in shops and factories. More and more immigrants (people from other countries), especially from Germany and Ireland, came to the Northern cities to do the same work. The North's economy depended on industry and manufacturing. This also made the North different from the South.

Many people in the North decided that slavery was wrong. By the early 1800s, most Northern states had abolished, or banned, slavery. Slavery was illegal in the states north of a line called the Mason-Dixon Line. South of the Mason-Dixon Line, slavery was legal. Long before the Civil War, slavery had divided the nation.

*New York City's Broadway bustled with activity in 1861.*

Northern workers leaving a factory at the end of the day, left. Southerners pointed to places in the North where white men, women, and child workers suffered from very long hours and faced many dangers from accidents. Many Southerners felt that black slaves lived a better life than did Northern workers.

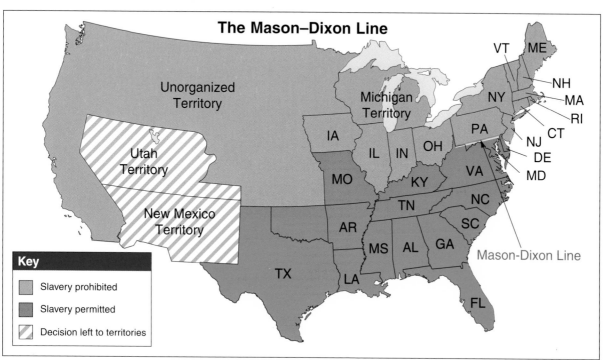

**The Mason–Dixon Line**

Unorganized Territory

Utah Territory

New Mexico Territory

Michigan Territory

IA

IL   IN   OH

MO   KY

TN

AR

MS   AL   GA

TX

LA

FL

SC

NC

VA

PA

NY

VT   ME

NH

MA

RI

CT

NJ

DE

MD

Mason-Dixon Line

**Key**

Slavery prohibited

Slavery permitted

Decision left to territories

# LIFE AS A SLAVE

In the 1930s, the U.S. government hired writers to interview more than two thousand former slaves about their lives during the time of slavery. In 1937 the people interviewed were old, but they were the only living people who remembered what it had been like to live as slaves. Every word they said was collected in a set of books called The American Slave. Here are some of the memories they shared:

ESTHER KING CASEY, former Alabama slave, recalling her master: *Captain King was a fine man. He treated all of us just like his own family. The white lady taught us to be respectable and truthful.*

AMY CHAPMAN, former Alabama slave, recalling an overseer (supervisor): *He was the meanest overseer we ever had. . . . That overseer was the first one that ever put me in the field, and he whupped me with the cat-o'-nine-tails [a whip] when I was stark naked.*

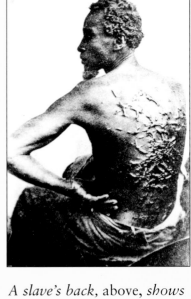

*A slave's back*, above, *shows the scars of many beatings.*

*Slaves had no legal rights. Therefore, their owners could treat them however they wanted*, left.

MARY CRANE, former Kentucky slave, recalling slave auctions: *In those days there were men who made a business of buying up negroes at auction sales and shipping them down to New Orleans to be sold to owners of cotton and sugar plantations. ... This practice gave rise to the expression "sold down the river"* [or, headed for rough times].

A slave merchant's advertisement

CARL BOONE, former Kentucky slave: *Master Thompson became angry, tied his slave to a whipping post and beat him terribly. Mrs. Thompson begged him to quit whipping, saying, "you might kill him," and the master replied that he aimed to kill him.*

LAURA CLARK, former Alabama slave: *When I was about six or seven years old. . . Mr. Garrett. . . bought ten of us children in North Carolina and sent two white men to fetch us back in wagons. . . . None of them ten children no kin to me, and he never bought my mammy, so I had to leave her behind. . . . I never seed her no more in this life.*

DELIA GARLIC, former Alabama slave: *I never seed none of my brothers and sisters except brother William. Him and my mother and me was brought . . . to Richmond and put in a warehouse. . . . Then we was all put on a block* [at auction] *and sold to the highest bidder. I never seed brother William again.*

13

# CHAPTER TWO

# Which Way to Grow?

In the 1800s, the United States expanded to the west. The expansion began in 1803, when the United States bought vast new lands from France. Most of the new land lay west of the Mississippi River. This area was known as the Louisiana Purchase. When a new state in this area joined the Union (the United States), the U.S. Congress had to make a decision. Should the new state be a free state or a slave state? Should the people in the new state be forbidden or allowed to own slaves?

The Constitution of the United States says that each state may elect two senators to the U.S. Senate. Before the Civil War, the North and the

*American families moved into the new western territories because they wanted to own land. They were willing to work hard for a chance at wealth.*

# ONE EVENING IN WASHINGTON

One evening in Washington, D.C., in 1820, U.S. Secretary of State John Quincy Adams walked home with John Calhoun. Adams came from Massachusetts. Calhoun was a very powerful congressman from South Carolina. The two men talked. That night Adams wrote down their conversation in his diary. Their words show that people in the North and the South thought very differently about slavery and about work.

Calhoun explained that, in the South, only certain kinds of work were fit for whites. Whites could farm or work in factories. But certain work, such as digging ditches or harvesting cotton, was "the proper work of slaves. No white person could descend to that."

*John Quincy Adams*

Adams told Calhoun that he "could not see things in the same light." Adams could not see why the type of work made any difference. Digging a ditch was hard work, but it was honest work. He thought that both whites and blacks alike should be able to do honest work.

Adams concluded that Calhoun was making an excuse for slavery. He wrote in his diary, "What can be more false and heartless than this doctrine which makes the first and holiest right [freedom] of humanity depend upon the color of the skin?"

*John Calhoun*

South wanted to make sure each side had the same number of senators. Otherwise, each side feared the other would take control of the Senate. They wanted a balance of senators from free states and from slave states.

To keep the balance, the U.S. Congress made a compromise, an agreement in which neither side got everything it wanted. The compromise divided the Louisiana Purchase east to west. New states to the north of this line entered the Union as free states. New states to the south of the line entered as slave states.

Missouri, which lay to the north of the line, was one exception. In 1821 the U.S. Congress allowed it to enter the Union as a slave state. This decision was known as the Missouri Compromise. Congressmen

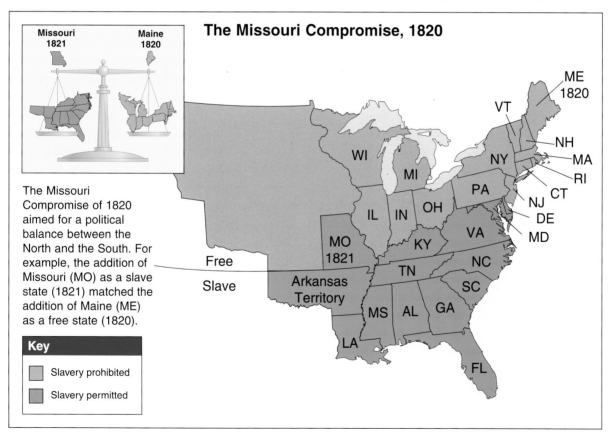

**The Missouri Compromise, 1820**

The Missouri Compromise of 1820 aimed for a political balance between the North and the South. For example, the addition of Missouri (MO) as a slave state (1821) matched the addition of Maine (ME) as a free state (1820).

**Key**

- Slavery prohibited
- Slavery permitted

*At slave auctions,* above, slaveholders inspected the "merchandise." They felt the slaves' muscles and looked at their teeth, just as they would inspect a farm animal. The strongest and most skilled slaves sometimes sold for more than one thousand dollars.

accepted the compromise to avoid a civil war. Secretary of State John Quincy Adams remarked, "If the Union must be dissolved [ended], slavery is precisely the question upon which it ought to break. For the present, however, this contest is laid asleep."

With the Missouri Compromise, slavery "laid asleep" until the mid-1800s. At that time, a great antislavery movement began. This movement was part of the Second Great Awakening, a religious movement that swept across the entire country. People in many parts of the country called for moral and cultural reform, or change. They believed that all people, whether white or black, were equal in God's sight. To end slavery, they voted for politicians who agreed that slavery was evil. These politicians and their supporters were known as abolitionists—people who wanted to abolish, or end, slavery in the United States.

Yet Southern planters who owned slaves, about one man in three, did not think of themselves as evil. They went to church and worshiped the same God as the abolitionists. They believed that slavery was a good thing. Slaveowners explained that the South was prosperous and peaceful because of slavery. They said that if slaves were emancipated, or freed, black people would fall into poverty and crime.

*From 1846 to 1848, while the issue of slavery was being discussed, the United States was fighting a war with Mexico. Americans understood that the results of the war would be very important to the future of the country.*

In 1848 the United States won a war with Mexico and gained "an immense empire" including modern-day Arizona, New Mexico, Utah, Nevada, and California, as well as parts of Colorado, Wyoming, and Texas. Again Congress debated whether or not to allow slavery in these new lands.

This debate led to new political parties, or groups. Old political parties stated their views more forcefully. John Calhoun from South Carolina presented the view of the slaveholders. He said that, according to the U.S. Constitution, slavery could not be banned in the new U.S. territories. Some Southern states threatened to secede, or leave the Union, if they did not get their way.

The abolitionists disagreed. But few abolitionists were elected to the U.S. Congress, so they were not very powerful. An Ohio politician named Salmon Chase helped form a new party called the Free Soil Party. Free Soilers believed that people who lived on new U.S. lands (or, U.S. soil) should be free and not slaves. The Free Soilers and the abolitionists joined together against slavery in the new U.S. territories.

Others believed that the decision to be a free or a slave state should be left up to the people who settled the new lands. Still others wanted to extend the line set by the Missouri Compromise farther west. There were so many groups and so many opinions that it seemed likely civil war (a war between citizens of one country) would break out.

To preserve the Union, two old and respected statesmen stepped forward in 1850. Kentuckian

*Salmon P. Chase, above, was a lawyer and politician who helped found the Free Soil Party.*

Henry Clay, aged seventy-two, urged a compromise. He would have failed without Daniel Webster, a sixty-eight-year-old from Massachusetts. Together they presented a compromise that made no one happy but kept the nation

## HENRY CLAY AND DANIEL WEBSTER

Henry Clay, *right,* born in Virginia in 1777, was known as "The Great Compromiser." Clay did not like slavery and hoped to see it ended. He did own slaves, but he freed them in his will. Henry Clay ran against John Quincy Adams for president in 1824 and lost. He served many years as a U.S. congressman and senator.

Daniel Webster, *left,* also spent many years as a U.S. congressman and senator. He also ran unsuccessfully for the U.S. presidency and then served as secretary of state for two different presidents. Webster was a great orator, or public speaker. He became famous for saying, "Liberty and Union, now and forever, one and inseparable!"

whole. The Compromise of 1850 allowed California to join the United States as a free state. It banned slavery in the District of Columbia, the nation's capital. It gave the new territories in Utah and New Mexico the right to decide for themselves whether to allow slavery. It also toughened the Fugitive Slave Law.

The Compromise of 1850 was the first of several political crises that took place over the next few years. The new U.S. territories became political battlegrounds between supporters of the South and supporters of the North.

*After the United States won the war with Mexico in 1848, the U.S. Congress had to decide whether to allow slavery in the new land won from Mexico. The Compromise of 1850 tried to divide up the land in a way that would prevent a civil war.*

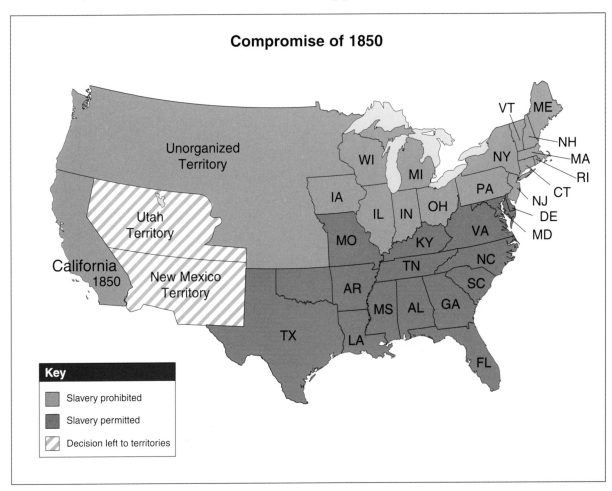

**Compromise of 1850**

Key
- Slavery prohibited
- Slavery permitted
- Decision left to territories

# THE FUGITIVE SLAVE LAW
## OF 1850

The Fugitive Slave Law of 1850 allowed slaveholders from the South to come North and recapture fugitive, or escaped, slaves. The new law was an important part of the Compromise of 1850, designed to appeal to the South.

Under the law, a slaveowner would tell a government official that he owned a black person who was living in the North. When the black person, the "fugitive," was found, he or she had to prove that he or she was free. Yet blacks were not allowed to testify or have a jury trial, which made this task nearly impossible. In the ten-year period after the law was passed, 332 blacks claimed by former owners were returned to slavery. Only 11 were allowed to remain free. Some slaveholders tried to capture people they claimed had escaped and lived in freedom for more than twenty years.

## $200 Reward.
### RANAWAY from the subscriber, on the night of Thursday, the 30th of Sepember.
## FIVE NEGRO SLAVES,

To-wit: one Negro man, his wife, and three children. The man is a black negro, full height, very erect, his face a little thin. He is about forty years of age, and calls himself *Washington Reed,* and is known by the name of Washington. He is probably well dressed, possibly takes with him an ivory headed cane, and is of good address. Several of his teeth are gone.

*Mary,* his wife, is about thirty years of age, a bright mulatto woman, and quite stout and strong.

The oldest of the children is a boy, of the name of FIELDING, twelve years of age, a dark mulatto, with heavy eyelids. He probably wore a new cloth cap.

MATILDA, the second child, is a girl, six years of age, rather a dark mulatto, but a bright and smart looking child.

MALCOLM, the youngest, is a boy, four years old, a lighter mulatto than the last, and about equally as bright. He probably also wore a cloth cap. If examined, he will be found to have a swelling at the navel.

Washington and Mary have lived at or near St. Louis, with the subscriber, for about 15 years. It is supposed that they are making their way to Chicago, and that a white man accompanies them, that they will travel chiefly at night, and most probably in a covered wagon.

A reward of $150 will be paid for their apprehension, so that I can get them, if taken within one hundred miles of St. Louis, and $200 if taken beyond that, and secured so that I can get them, and other reasonable additional charges, if delivered to the subscriber, or to THOMAS ALLEN, Esq., at St. Louis, Mo. The above negroes, for the last few years, have been in possession of Thomas Allen, Esq., of St. Louis.

ST. LOUIS, Oct. 1, 1847.

## WM. RUSSELL.

*Owners often advertised for the return of runaway slaves.*

23

# CHAPTER THREE

# Growing Apart

In 1854 a Democratic senator from Illinois named Stephen A. Douglas proposed a law to form two new territories—Kansas and Nebraska. His proposal was known as the Kansas-Nebraska Act. It was one of the most important events that pushed the nation into civil war.

Douglas wanted to encourage settlers to move west. He also wanted the United States to have a railroad from the Atlantic Ocean to the Pacific Ocean. To build a railroad, the land had to have defined boundaries. To create boundaries, new territories were formed. But everyone knew that creating new territories was the first step toward creating new states. Kansas and Nebraska were located where the Missouri Compromise had banned slavery. It seemed certain that when the new territories became states, they would be free states.

Southern senators could not accept this. But Douglas needed their support to have Congress pass his law. To please the Southern senators, Douglas proposed that the settlers of Kansas and Nebraska

*Stephen Douglas,* right

*This cartoonish illustration,* left, *shows how many Southerners saw slave life. But the cottage is far nicer than most slave cabins, and slaves rarely had time, or even permission, to dance.*

make their own decisions about slavery. Douglas was small, standing only five feet four inches tall. But he was a forceful person. He earned the nickname the "Little Giant." The Little Giant convinced enough politicians to vote his way, and Congress passed the Kansas-Nebraska Act into law. The new law destroyed the Missouri Compromise, an agreement that had held the nation together for thirty-four years.

Free Soiler Salmon Chase called the new law a "gross violation of a sacred pledge." Across the North, people met at hundreds of "anti-Nebraska" meetings to protest the new law. Northern voters formed many new political parties, all of them against slavery. One of the

*The Kansas-Nebraska Act let settlers of the two territories decide for themselves about slavery.*

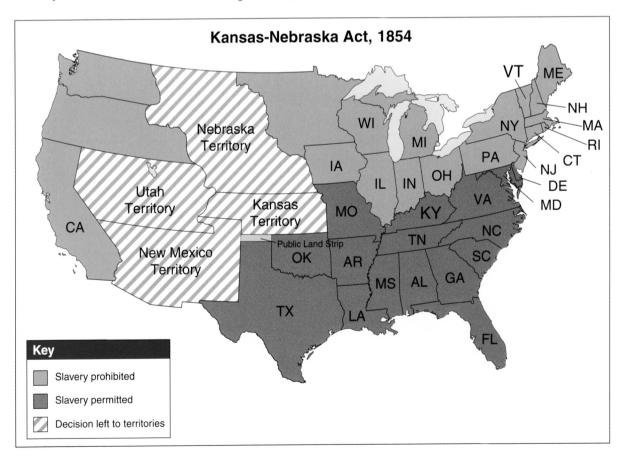

**Kansas-Nebraska Act, 1854**

VT
ME
NH
MA
RI
CT
NJ
DE
MD
NY
PA
VA
WI
MI
IA
IL IN OH
KY
NC
MO
TN
SC
Nebraska Territory
Public Land Strip
OK
AR
MS AL GA
Utah Territory
Kansas Territory
CA
New Mexico Territory
TX
LA
FL

**Key**
- Slavery prohibited
- Slavery permitted
- Decision left to territories

*Some political meetings, like this one in New York City, drew such big crowds that they were held outdoors.*

most important new parties was the Republican Party.

Politicians running for office in 1854 fought tough, bitter campaigns, especially in Douglas's home state of Illinois. Politicians relied on their ability to speak at public gatherings to convince voters to support them. They stood above the crowd on stages, platforms, wagons, or even tree stumps to be seen and heard. Crowds expected the politicians to entertain them with witty remarks and to talk about the great issues of the day. Douglas, a Democrat, was very good at this. But another politician, a Republican, was even better. His name was Abraham Lincoln.

In 1854 Lincoln was little known outside of Illinois. But, as Lincoln said, the Kansas-Nebraska Act "aroused" him "as he had never been before." He went to Springfield, the capital of Illinois, to challenge Douglas. Lincoln waited until after

*Lincoln's reputation as an honest person led one enthusiastic supporter to write a song about him.*

Douglas had given a speech. As people were leaving, they saw Lincoln standing on the staircase to the stage. Lincoln said that he wanted to speak the next day. He invited Douglas to attend. So people came back the next day to hear Lincoln speak about slavery. In the front row sat Douglas.

It was a hot October day. Soon Lincoln was wet with sweat, his shirt clinging to his shoulders and long arms. He was not a handsome man, but his words were beautiful to hear. For the first time, Lincoln explained the ideas that would eventually carry him to the White House as president of the United States. He spoke about a doctrine, or idea, that was at the heart of the American system. He said, "If the Negro is a man, why then my ancient faith teaches me that 'all men are created equal,' and that there can be no moral right in connection with one man's making a slave of another." Lincoln believed that black people were humans and not property owned by a master.

Lincoln felt that no act of Congress could deny this truth. If all men are created equal, then slavery is wrong. Newspapers reported Lincoln's words, and his speech caused him to become well known.

# ABRAHAM LINCOLN

Abraham Lincoln was born in Kentucky on February 12, 1809. Lincoln's father was a carpenter and farmer. Neither of his parents knew how to read or write. Young Abraham worked hard during his childhood. At the age of seven, he helped to put up his family's log cabin in Indiana.

Lincoln's mother Nancy died when he was only nine. She died of "milk sickness," which was caused by drinking milk from cows that had eaten poisonous plants. Lincoln's father married again. Sarah, his new wife, treated Abraham very kindly and encouraged him to learn. He was fond of her all his life. Abraham went to school only now and then, probably not even a total of one year in his whole life. But he learned to read, write, and do arithmetic, mostly by studying on his own.

Lincoln stood six feet four inches tall and was very thin. But all the hard work of a frontier farm had made him a strong man. He was pleasant company and knew how to tell funny stories. At the age of twenty-one, Lincoln helped his family move to Illinois and start a new farm. Then he went out on his own and worked at many different jobs. In his spare time, he studied to become a lawyer.

Lincoln joined the U.S. Army in 1832. He was elected captain of his company but never did any fighting. Later in 1832, Lincoln decided to start out in politics by running for the Illinois state assembly, but he lost. He tried again and won the first of many political victories in 1834.

When he was thirty-three years old, Lincoln married Mary Todd. They had four sons, one of whom died as a baby.

# CHAPTER FOUR

# The Violence Begins

The Kansas-Nebraska Act brought national attention to Abraham Lincoln. But in Kansas, the act brought extreme violence. The Kansas-Nebraska Act allowed settlers living in Kansas to decide if Kansas would become a free state or a slave state. Kansas settlers disagreed so forcefully that they fought with gun, knife, and fire. The violence was so horrible that Kansas became known as "Bleeding Kansas."

The abolitionists knew the decision about Kansas was important to saving the Union. Senator William H. Seward, an abolitionist leader from New York, promised to fight for Kansas as a free state. He knew that Northerners outnumbered Southerners. Seward said, "God give the victory to the side which is stronger in numbers as it is in right."

Proslavery leaders also knew the battle for Kansas was important. A Missouri senator named David Atchison said, "We are playing for a mighty stake. . . . If we win we carry slavery to the Pacific Ocean." He thought that supporters of slavery could win by terrorizing abolitionists. "We will be compelled to shoot, burn & hang, but the thing will soon be over." He was right about the violence. But the struggle for Kansas did not end quickly.

The decision depended on Kansas voters. So both sides sent their supporters to live in Kansas. A proslavery Kansas newspaper declared: "Come on, Southern men! Bring your slaves and fill up the Territory." At the same time, settlers

*A Free State Battery, below, in Kansas. The fighting in Kansas became a battle between abolitionists and proslavery forces. Armed units, including Free State Batteries, began organizing around 1856 to fight on the side of the antislavery settlers.*

*Senator Charles Sumner did not fully recover for three years from the injuries caused by his beating.*

came from the North carrying weapons bought for them by wealthy New England abolitionists.

During the spring of 1856, skirmishes, or small fights, broke out in many places in Kansas. Lawrence was the center of Kansas's free state movement. Proslavery leaders decided to attack the village.

A proslavery judge sent a posse (a group of armed men) to arrest the abolitionist leaders who lived in Lawrence. Dragging five cannons, the posse surrounded Lawrence. Inside Lawrence, the abolitionists decided not to fight back. About eight hundred members of the posse entered the town to burn and rob. They destroyed two newspaper offices and burned the home of a well-known antislavery leader.

In the North, abolitionists pointed to Lawrence as an example of proslavery people destroying citizens' rights. In Congress, politicians argued back and forth. They felt so strongly that violence occurred even in the nation's Capitol building.

A senator from Massachusetts named Charles Sumner was well known throughout the nation for his antislavery views. After Lawrence was attacked, Sumner delivered a two-day speech at the Capitol. He called his speech "The Crime Against Kansas." Sumner spoke strongly against what had happened in Kansas. In his speech, he also insulted several Southern congressmen.

Two days later, Preston Brooks, a congressman from South Carolina, took revenge. He walked up to the desk in the Capitol building where

Sumner was writing a letter and beat him over the head with a gold-headed cane. Sumner recovered, but his beating was a blow against the American tradition of free speech and the rule of law.

Yet many Southerners treated Brooks like a hero. South Carolina newspapers praised Brooks for his defense of the state's honor. *The Richmond Enquirer* agreed, saying, "The vulgar Abolitionists in the Senate. . . should be lashed into submission." From places all over the South, people sent Brooks new canes on which they wrote such things as "Hit Him Again."

Northerners were shocked by the South's response to Sumner's beating. They wondered whether the United States really could be a united nation with some states free and others slave.

*After the massacre at Pottawatomie Creek, John Brown said, "I have only a short time to live—only one death to die—and I will die fighting for this cause. There will be no more peace in this land until slavery is done for."*

Brooks's attack on Sumner showed how difficult it would be for political leaders to continue to compromise.

When news of Brooks's actions reached Kansas, a fifty-six-year-old abolitionist went "crazy" with anger. John Brown had dedicated his life to ending slavery. In the spring of 1856, he and several of his sons went to Lawrence to help defend against proslavery forces. Brown was a strong, convincing speaker. He urged the people of Kansas to "fight fire with fire" and to "strike terror into the hearts of the proslavery people."

Brown gathered a small group near his home. During the night, they stalked up to the cabins of five proslavery men at Pottawatomie Creek, kidnapped them, and killed them.

Brown escaped punishment for this massacre. The killings encouraged the proslavery forces in Kansas to fight back. Kansas became a battleground with hit-and-run raids, ambushes, and murder in the night. This was Bleeding Kansas.

In 1857 the judges of the U.S. Supreme Court made a proslavery decision that continued to widen the gap between North and South. A slave named Dred Scott sued for his freedom. Scott and his family had lived with their owner, an army surgeon, in the state of Illinois and in the territory of Minnesota, where slavery was forbidden. But their owner's home state, Missouri, was a slave state.

To make a decision, the Supreme Court had to answer four questions. Could a black man be considered a full American citizen with the right to sue? Did two years living in a free state (Illinois) plus two years in a free territory (Minnesota) make a slave free? Was the territory in which Scott lived actually free? More important, did the U.S. government have the right to ban slavery in a territory that had not yet become a state?

*Dred Scott,* above right, *first sued for freedom in Missouri for himself, his wife,* above left, *and his family in 1846. The 1857 U.S. Supreme Court decision was the end to a long legal struggle.*

At this time, the Supreme Court had more judges from the South than from the North. It was no surprise that the Court decided that blacks were not American citizens and had no right to sue. The judges argued that the writers of the Declaration of Independence had not meant to include blacks when they declared that all men were created equal. The Court also stated that the U.S. Congress had no right to ban slavery in the territories.

The Supreme Court's decision caused an uproar in the North. Americans realized that the conflict over slavery would not be settled through the legal system. Shortly after the Supreme Court decision, Dred Scott's owner freed him. Scott died a year later, but his name lives on.

In 1858 Abraham Lincoln and Stephen Douglas faced off again. Both wanted to become a senator for Illinois. During the campaign, the two men met in a series of public debates. Douglas wore fine clothes and gestured dramatically when he spoke. Lincoln wore a plain black suit and spoke in a high, sharp voice. But people did not care what the rivals looked like. They gathered in crowds of ten to fifteen thousand to listen to the words of the two men.

Lincoln stated that the past five years of compromise on slavery had not worked. In fact, compromise had failed badly. The nation was still bitterly divided. Lincoln claimed that problems would grow worse if compromise continued. He said, "A house divided against

*In the days before television, people loved to go out and hear politicians debate the important issues of the day. Abraham Lincoln, at podium, and Stephen Douglas, behind Lincoln, were both excellent speakers and attracted great crowds.*

itself cannot stand. I believe this government cannot endure permanently half slave and half free. I do not expect the Union to be dissolved; I do not expect the house to fall; but I do expect it will cease to be divided. It will become all one thing, or all the other."

Douglas and other Democrats felt that Lincoln's words were too radical and that he was too willing to risk civil war. Illinois voters agreed, and they elected Douglas to the Senate. Lincoln accepted his defeat with grace. He knew that his fame was growing because of his debates with Douglas. He knew that he had a good chance to become the next Republican presidential candidate. Lincoln worked to improve his chances. Then, in mid-October 1859, John Brown struck again.

*Harpers Ferry, Virginia, in the 1800s. The village stands at the place where two rivers, the Shenandoah and the Potomac, meet.*

36

Brown planned to conduct a raid to capture weapons stored at an arsenal (warehouse) in Harpers Ferry, Virginia. Brown had become impatient with the nation's lack of progress at ending slavery. After a meeting of the New England Anti-Slavery Society, he complained that "[All abolitionists do is] Talk! Talk! Talk! That will never free the slaves. What is needed is action—action." After stealing the weapons, Brown planned to move into the rugged mountains of western Virginia. He believed that slaves would join him there. He would then give them weapons. His goal was to trigger a slave uprising that would spread across the South.

Brown's idea was not well thought out or wise. But he was a deeply religious man who told his followers that "one man and God can overturn the universe." Brown tried to convince his friend Frederick Douglass—an important black leader in the North—to join him, but Douglass refused. Douglass believed that the raid would fail. He warned that Brown would "never get out alive."

With an army of seventeen whites and five blacks, Brown surprised guards and captured weapons at Harpers Ferry on the night of October 16, 1859. The alarm spread rapidly. By midmorning on October 18, armed citizens from Virginia and Maryland had driven Brown and his followers into a thick-walled fire-engine house. Surrounded and trapped, Brown prepared for a last stand.

Meanwhile, in Washington, D.C., military authorities called an officer named Robert Edward Lee to headquarters. Lee received orders to take a company of U.S. Marines to Harpers Ferry and arrest Brown.

The marines stormed the engine house. They killed two raiders and captured the others, including Brown. In just thirty-six hours, John Brown's raid was over.

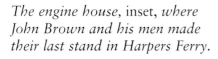

*The engine house,* inset, *where John Brown and his men made their last stand in Harpers Ferry.*

*With Lieutenant J. E. B. Stuart serving under him, Robert E. Lee led a company of marines against Brown,* lower right, *at Harpers Ferry.*

John Brown's trial was a national sensation. In the South, and especially in Virginia, mobs gathered to demand Brown's death. In the North, many abolitionists praised Brown's effort. Leaders in Virginia feared violence, so they quickly tried and convicted Brown of treason and murder. A Virginia judge sentenced Brown to hang on December 2, 1859.

An eyewitness to the execution, Thomas J. Jackson, wrote that Brown "behaved with unflinching firmness" during the execution. After the hanging, a jailer found a note that Brown had left behind. It read, "I, John Brown, am now quite certain that the crimes of this guilty land will never be purged away but with blood."

*John Brown—who had been wounded during his capture—was carried to his trial on a stretcher.*

# CHAPTER FIVE

# One Nation Becomes Two

Forty years of compromise between North and South had failed. The final crisis came in 1860, an election year. Four honorable men representing four different ideas about the future of the nation competed to become president of the United States.

The Democrats held their convention in Charleston, South Carolina. Outside the convention hall, speakers made fiery speeches about states' rights, slavery, and honor. Inside the hall, politicians in two opposing factions (groups)

*The South Carolina Institute, where the Democratic party held its convention in 1860*

*The site of the 1860 Republican national convention was in Chicago, Illinois.*

tried to choose a candidate. One faction supported the proslavery John C. Breckinridge, the current vice president of the United States. The other faction supported Stephen Douglas.

The Republicans met in Chicago. Like the Democrats, the Republicans were divided. Four candidates competed to become the Republican candidate for president. Abraham Lincoln was the strongest candidate. People trusted Lincoln and nicknamed him "Honest Abe." When the Republican Party selected Lincoln to be its candidate, it chose a man with many strengths and few weaknesses.

In addition to Breckinridge, Douglas, and Lincoln, a fourth candidate was John Bell of Tennessee. He represented a new party called the

Constitutional Union Party. The Constitutional Union Party took no stand at all on slavery and other major issues. Instead, it pledged "to recognize no political principle other than the Constitution . . . the Union . . . and the Enforcement of the Laws." These were high-sounding words. They appealed to many people who feared civil war. But many voters also wondered what such a party would do about the serious issues that divided the nation.

At the start of the campaign, Douglas appeared to have a real chance to win. Presidential candidates at this time remained silent during a campaign. Lincoln followed this tradition. Douglas boldly did not. Even though he was gravely ill, he traveled throughout the country. He carried the message that he was the only leader who could keep the country united. It was a courageous effort that exhausted him and did much to bring on his death the next year. But it was not enough. Lincoln won the election.

Lincoln's election marked a turning point. A Richmond, Virginia, newspaper gloomily wrote, "A party founded on the single sentiment . . . of hatred of African slavery, is now the controlling power." A New Orleans, Louisiana, paper described the Republicans as a revolutionary party. Antislavery people agreed that the election marked a revolution. "We live in revolutionary times," wrote an Illinois man. "I say God bless the revolution." No one could yet see that Lincoln's election would lead to a terrible, bloody civil war.

*From a pair of old fence rails he had supposedly split, Abraham Lincoln earned the nickname "The Railsplitter." With this nickname, Lincoln became a symbol of many things that Americans valued greatly: the frontier, the farm, and hard work.*

43

The conflict began in South Carolina. That state had promised to secede, or leave the Union, if Lincoln won the election. On December 20, 1860, it did. By March 1861, Mississippi, Florida, Alabama, Georgia, Louisiana, and Texas had also seceded. These states formed a confederation, or group, called the Confederate States of America (the Confederacy). Leaders of the Confederacy chose a man named Jefferson Davis to be the president of their new nation.

Two weeks before Lincoln's inauguration (the official beginning of a president's duties), the Confederacy held its own inauguration.

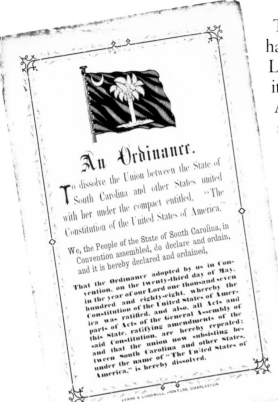

*South Carolina's Ordinance of Secession*, above. *An ordinance is a government order or law.*

*The illustration*, right, *is a political cartoon from 1860. The baby is a symbol of the United States, which was a young nation at this time. The baby is strangling the forces of secession, which are shown as snakes.*

44

*Before he became president of the Confederacy, Jefferson Davis had a long career of service to the United States as a soldier and a politician.*

## JEFFERSON DAVIS

Jefferson Davis was born on a farm in Kentucky in 1808. He was the youngest of ten children.

Davis attended the U.S. Military Academy at West Point in New York. He graduated from West Point in 1828 and spent four and a half years in the U.S. Army.

Davis eventually left the army and married Sarah Knox Taylor. Davis's older brother Joseph gave the couple part of his plantation and sold them fourteen slaves. A few months later, Sarah died of malaria. Davis also got malaria, but he survived. His friends said the loss of his wife changed him, making him unsociable and uninterested in life.

After seven years of keeping to himself, Davis met and married eighteen-year-old Varina Howell. He became interested in politics and was elected to the U.S. House of Representatives in 1845. When war with Mexico broke out in 1846, Davis led soldiers into battle and showed great courage. Davis's new reputation as a war hero helped him to be elected a U.S. senator. Davis was fifty-three years old when he became president of the Confederacy.

*The 1861 inauguration of Jefferson Davis as president of the Confederate States of America. Davis did not want to be president. His wife said that when he got the news that he was to be president, "he looked so grieved that I feared some evil had befallen our family."*

In his inaugural speech in Montgomery, Alabama, Jefferson Davis calmly spoke of the new nation. He showed no interest in rejoining the North. He said that the new Confederate nation faced uncertain times. But he had confidence that Southerners were willing to make whatever sacrifices necessary to preserve "honor and right and liberty and equality." Davis believed that the Confederate States of America represented the true principles of the United States's founding fathers, such as George Washington and Thomas Jefferson.

Confederate leaders copied the language of the U.S. Constitution in their new constitution. "We, the people of the United States" became "We, the people of the Confederate States, each state acting in its sovereign and independent character." From its birth, the Confederacy was founded on the rights of individual states instead of the rights of a federal, or national, government.

The most important difference between the U.S. Constitution and the Confederate Constitution was slavery. The Confederate Constitution stated plainly that slavery was to be "recognized and

*The citizens of Savannah, Georgia, displayed a specially designed flag declaring their independence.*

protected." Slavery would be allowed in western territories of the Confederate States of America.

Jefferson Davis and other secessionist leaders had formed a new nation. Davis believed that with "the God of our fathers to guide and protect us" the Confederate States of America would triumph. If it required a war to preserve it, so be it.

Americans in both North and South anxiously waited to learn what Lincoln intended to do. The day finally came for Lincoln to depart his home in Illinois for Washington, D.C. His neighbors gathered to say good-bye. Lincoln told them, "My friends, no one not in my situation can appreciate my feeling of sadness at this parting. To this place and the kindness of these people I owe everything. Here I have lived for a quarter of a century, and have passed from a young to an old man. Here my children have been born, and one is buried. I now leave, not knowing when, or whether ever, I may return, with a task before me greater than that which rested upon [George] Washington."

Lincoln placed his faith in God. "With that assistance, I cannot fail. Trusting in Him who can go with me, and remain with you, and be everywhere for good, let us confidently hope that all will yet be well." Lincoln bid his neighbors and friends farewell and boarded the train. His stepmother, with whom he shared a very close relationship, remembered his departure. "I knowed when he went away he wasn't ever coming back alive."

Lincoln knew that the entire nation, especially the Southern states, would listen carefully to the words he spoke at his inauguration. He had worked on his speech for months. His first words were spoken for Southern ears. He said that he wouldn't end slavery in the

states where it already existed. But he said that no state had the right to break away from the Union.

Lincoln explained that a president's most important duty was to see that the laws of the Union be faithfully carried out. Lincoln pledged "to preserve, protect, and defend" the United States. He called Southerners "my dissatisfied fellow countrymen" and said that "the momentous issue of civil war" was in their hands. The government would not attack them. War would only come if they attacked first.

In Montgomery, Alabama, President Jefferson Davis had spoken about the future of the Confederacy. In Washington, D.C., President Abraham Lincoln spoke about the future of the Union. Both men knew that the future depended on the actions of eight states: Virginia, North Carolina, Tennessee, Arkansas, Delaware, Maryland, Kentucky, and Missouri. These states were neutral—they had not made up their minds which side to join.

Lincoln wanted the neutral states to remain part of the United States. Davis wanted the neutral states to become part of the Confederacy. But Lincoln and Davis were very careful as they worked to convince the states to choose a side. Neither president wanted his side to become the aggressor (the side that starts a war).

Lincoln knew that many Northerners did not want to use force to keep the states united. But Lincoln knew that force would probably be necessary. How could he convince the Northerners to support the use of force? One way was to force the Southerners to attack first. If the Southerners were the aggressors, Lincoln believed that Northerners would defend themselves.

*The U.S. Capitol building under construction in 1860*

CHAPTER SIX

# First Shots at Fort Sumter

Northerners, called Yankees in the South, controlled four forts in the South. Southerners thought that they should control these forts. Rebels in South Carolina did not like seeing the U.S. flag flying over Fort Sumter, in Charleston Harbor. They decided to capture the fort.

After their state seceded, South Carolina rebels placed artillery (guns and cannons) around Charleston Harbor and at Fort Moultrie, which faced Fort Sumter from the east. The artillery prevented ships from bringing food and other supplies to Fort Sumter. The Southerners hoped that U.S. soldiers would run out of food and surrender without a battle. Both sides waited. Neither wanted to fire the first shot and be the one to begin a war.

On March 5, 1861, the day after his inauguration, Lincoln received a message from Major Robert Anderson, the officer who commanded

*Major Robert Anderson,* above, *commanded the soldiers at Fort Sumter. He was a slaveowner from Kentucky whose sympathies lay with the South. But his sense of duty to the United States compelled him to defend the fort.*

*Named after Thomas Sumter—a Southern hero of the American Revolution—Fort Sumter was a powerful fortress with walls forty feet high and eight to twelve feet thick. In 1861 forty-eight guns were mounted on the fort's walls.*

Fort Sumter. Anderson wrote that there was only enough food to last six weeks. Lincoln faced a major decision. Should he order ships to bring supplies to Fort Sumter? If he did, the South might attack his ships and the soldiers in the fort. Despite the risk, Lincoln decided to send the

*Charleston, South Carolina, in 1861,* below

supply ships. On April 6, Lincoln sent ships to Fort Sumter. He told the governor of South Carolina that the ships were carrying only food, not weapons. Lincoln hoped that Confederate leaders would not fire at a ship carrying food to hungry men.

Davis then had to make an important decision. Should he order his soldiers to attack Lincoln's ships and capture Fort Sumter? One of Davis's advisers, Robert Toombs, told Davis, "The firing on that fort will inaugurate [begin] a civil war greater than any the world has yet seen." But Davis and other Southern leaders believed their side was in the right. Davis ordered his soldiers to open fire on Fort Sumter.

At 4:30 on a Friday morning, April 12, 1861, the first gun fired. Soon forty-seven artillery pieces bombarded Fort Sumter. The Confederates fired heavy cannonballs that shattered the fort's stone walls. They also shot heated iron balls that

*The original Fort Sumter had five sides.*
1) *The wall facing Charleston*
2) *The wall facing Fort Moultrie, across the main ship channel*
3) *The wall facing the Atlantic Ocean*
4) *The wall facing the Confederate guns on Morris Island*
5) *The corner where Captain Abner Doubleday commanded a Federal (Union) gun crew. He became an important general later in the war.*
6) *Protective structures put up by Federal engineers as shields against rebel cannonballs*
7) *Sandbags to protect Union gunners from the Confederate guns at Fort Moultrie*

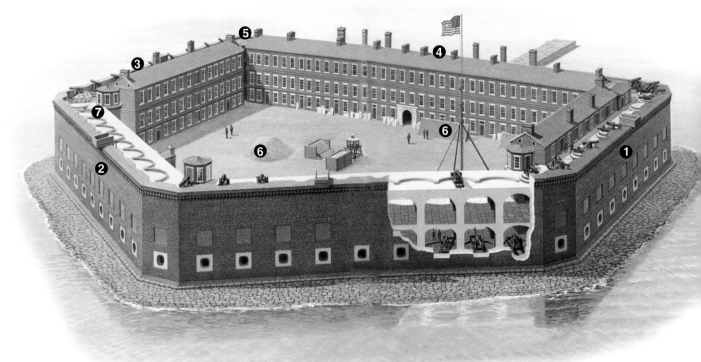

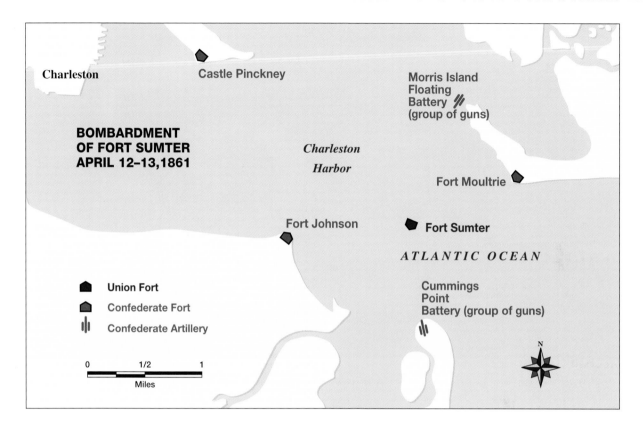

Charleston

Castle Pinckney

Morris Island
Floating
Battery
(group of guns)

**BOMBARDMENT
OF FORT SUMTER
APRIL 12–13,1861**

*Charleston*

*Harbor*

Fort Moultrie

Fort Johnson

Fort Sumter

*ATLANTIC OCEAN*

Cummings
Point
Battery (group of guns)

Union Fort

Confederate Fort

Confederate Artillery

0    1/2    1

Miles

N

set fire to the fort's wooden buildings. Inside the fort, the smoke was so thick that the defenders had to breathe through wet handkerchiefs. The soldiers inside the fort fired back, but they knew that the South was winning.

The battle continued all day Friday, on through the night, and into Saturday. Anderson's men could no longer defend the fort as it was being destroyed around them. They had put up enough of a fight to uphold their honor. Major Anderson surrendered the fort to the Confederates. Amazingly, no one had been injured during the fighting. But an accident after the surrender caused an explosion that killed a U.S. private named Daniel Hough. He was the first to die in a war that would claim more than 620,000 soldiers' lives.

Inside Fort Sumter, the Union defenders knew that the South was winning. But they kept shooting to show they could still fight, above.

Confederate gunners, right, pounded Fort Sumter with more than four thousand shots fired from cannons, howitzers, and mortars.

The attackers allowed the defeated Anderson and his men to safely board a ship. As it departed Charleston Harbor, Confederates stood on the beaches. They were silent and removed their hats to honor the courage of Fort Sumter's defenders.

The Civil War had begun. On April 15, 1861, Lincoln requested that 75,000 men enlist, or sign up, to fight against the Confederacy. This request excited the nation. Just as Lincoln had hoped, Northerners united against the South. Lincoln's old rival, Stephen Douglas, told a crowd in Chicago, "Every man must be for the United States or against it. There can be no neutrals in this war, only patriots or traitors." The citizens of New York City held a parade that brought out 250,000 people. The American flag, the Stars and Stripes, flew from nearly every house, dome, and

*Fort Moultrie*, below, *from where Confederate troops conducted the bombardment of Fort Sumter*

*The Confederate flag flying over Fort Sumter, right. The news of Fort Sumter traveled to the army posts in the west. An officer remembered the sad news that "lifelong friends" were firing at each other. He wrote, "All were quiet, serious and thoughtful, as we [went] back to our quarters to tell our wives and children that all our hopes of peace were blasted, and that our once happy and prosperous country was plunged into the horrors of civil war."*

steeple. One soldier, a veteran of a previous war, wrote, "Everything wore the aspect of a gala day, and the people seemed to be on one grand picnic." But this soldier knew that the citizens of New York would not be so excited if they knew how terrible war could be.

Northern states quickly enlisted more than 75,000. Lincoln asked Indiana for six regiments, and the governor offered twelve. Ohio's governor asked to send additional soldiers because so many men were volunteering.

The Southern states that had remained neutral reacted strongly against Lincoln's call for soldiers. Virginia, North Carolina, Tennessee, and Arkansas joined the Confederacy. The governor of Virginia charged that Lincoln had chosen to begin the war. The governor of Arkansas said that his people "will defend to the last . . . their honor, lives, and property" against the North. The vice president of the Confederacy, Alexander Stephens, cried, "Lincoln may bring his 75,000 troops against us. We fight for our homes, our fathers and mothers, our wives, brothers, sisters, sons, and daughters! We can call out a million of peoples if need be, and when they are cut down we can call another, and still another." Davis announced, "All we ask is to be let alone."

Delaware, Maryland, Kentucky, and Missouri still remained neutral. The governors of Delaware and Maryland were cautious about sending troops. They would wait and see what happened. The governor of Kentucky answered, "Kentucky will furnish no troops for the wicked purpose of subduing her sister Southern States." The Missouri governor called Lincoln's request for soldiers "illegal, unconstitutional, revolutionary, inhuman." He refused to send Missouri men to fight for Lincoln.

*The 6th Massachusetts marching into the railroad station in Jersey City, New Jersey. They were the first to respond to Lincoln's call for troops.*

Lincoln believed that Kentucky was the key. If it seceded from the Union and joined the Confederacy, Missouri and Maryland would follow. This would be disaster for the North. Lincoln told a friend that if Kentucky went with the South, the war was lost for the Union.

Meanwhile, the first group of soldiers, the 6th Massachusetts, entered Baltimore, Maryland, on its way to Washington, D.C., to protect the capital city. Baltimore was a pro-Southern city. A mob gathered and started throwing bricks at the soldiers. A few people fired pistols. The soldiers were angry and afraid. Some fired back, causing a riot. Four soldiers and twelve civilians (people who are not part of the military) died.

The 6th Massachusetts finally arrived in Washington, D.C. Behind it, Confederates cut

*Volunteer troops from Massachusetts (a Northern state) under attack by citizens of Baltimore, Maryland (a pro-Southern city)*

*The funeral in Boston of the four Massachusetts soldiers killed by a pro-Southern mob in Baltimore*

telegraph lines and burned railroad bridges. Several more days passed. The capital was almost defenseless. Lincoln looked outside the windows of the White House to see if any more Union soldiers had arrived. When he did not see them, he muttered, "Why don't they come? Why don't they come?" He looked across the Potomac River and saw the campfires of Confederate soldiers. It seemed like an attack could come at any moment.

Finally on Thursday, April 25, a locomotive's shrieking whistle announced the arrival of a train. It carried the 7th New York regiment. Following the 7th New York came 2,400 more soldiers from Rhode Island and Massachusetts. For the time being, the capital was safe.

Most Americans expected that the war would be over quickly. They figured that there would be only one battle. So both sides worked hard to be ready for this battle.

Ninety miles south of Washington, D.C., lay the Confederate capital at Richmond, Virginia. President Jefferson Davis ordered his army to guard Richmond. In the North, a clamor arose to end the war quickly by marching on Richmond. "On to Richmond!" was the cry.

One army would march on Richmond. Another army would block it. The collision came on the banks of a small creek in Virginia known as Bull Run. Instead of being the war's last battle, it became the first of many.

*The 7th New York marching down Broadway on their way to defend Washington, D.C.*

61

# The Abolitionists

In the years before the Civil War, beliefs about slavery led to many discussions and arguments in the United States. Americans learned about slavery by reading books and newspapers and by attending lectures by public speakers. *Abolitionist* was the word for people who wanted to abolish, or end, slavery. Many of the men and women who led the abolition movement became well known as speakers and writers. The stories of some abolitionists show how ordinary Americans worked to end slavery.

## The Farm Girl

ABBY KELLEY was born in 1810 and grew up on a farm in Worcester, Massachusetts. She became a schoolteacher and joined a female antislavery society. She was one of the first women to speak in public against slavery. She became well known as an abolitionist and also helped organize the first National Woman's Rights Convention in Worcester in 1850.

Abby Kelley was famous and outspoken, but she also worked with ordinary citizens to find ways to oppose slavery. She was a member of an antislavery sewing circle that included a few free black women. Women gathered together in sewing circles to share the work of sewing clothes for their families. At the same time, they talked about how to help end slavery. They began to sew clothing for escaped slaves. They also sold handmade items to raise money for the abolitionists.

## The Former Slaves

SOJOURNER TRUTH was born around 1797. (It is difficult to determine exactly when some slaves were born because written records of slaves' lives were usually not made.) She was a slave in New York until just before that state abolished slavery in 1827. She traveled around the country to speak against slavery. She was a powerful speaker who persuaded some listeners and enraged others.

*Harriet Tubman, opposite top, rescued more than three hundred black Americans from slavery. Because she led so many slaves to freedom, she was called the Moses of her people.*

*The Underground Railroad was a group of American citizens, both white and black, who secretly cooperated to help slaves escape to freedom, opposite bottom. The Underground Railroad was against the laws of the time, and members risked being arrested if they were caught.*

Sojourner Truth also spoke for women's rights in the 1850s. During the Civil War, she helped gather supplies for black soldiers. She became so famous that, in 1864, President Abraham Lincoln welcomed her to the White House. After the war, she helped ex-slaves to begin their new lives of freedom.

HARRIET TUBMAN, born around 1820, not only escaped from slavery herself but also went on to be a "conductor" on the Underground Railroad. The Underground Railroad was a secret route of hiding places across the country. This "railroad" did not use any trains. Members used railroad terms, such as "conductor," to describe those who led slaves, or "passengers," to safe hiding places, called "stations." Escaping slaves could rest at each stop before continuing the journey to freedom in the North or in Canada. She rescued more than three hundred black Americans from slavery, including her brothers, sisters, and parents. During the Civil War, Tubman helped the Union army as a nurse, laundress, and spy.

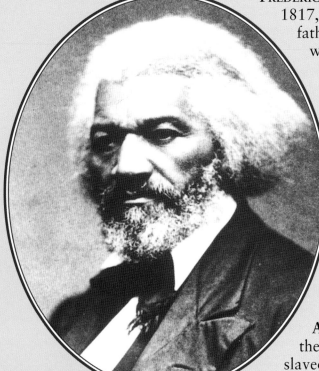

FREDERICK DOUGLASS was born in Maryland in 1817, to a slave mother and an unknown white father. He secretly learned to read and write, which was against the law for a slave. Douglass escaped to Massachusetts when he was a young man.

Douglass was a brilliant speaker and writer. He published an abolitionist paper called *North Star*. He worked as an abolitionist throughout the Civil War and organized two regiments of black soldiers in Massachusetts. He was sometimes insulted or attacked by people who disagreed with him, but he did not stop his work until the goal of freedom was achieved.

*When he escaped from slavery, Frederick Augustus Washington Bailey, above, changed his name to Frederick Douglass in order to avoid being caught.*

## The Planter's Daughters

ANGELINA AND SARAH GRIMKÉ grew up in the early 1800s as the daughters of a rich slaveowner in South Carolina. These two sisters were upset by what they saw on their father's plantation. They came to believe slavery was evil and should be abolished. They even dared to break the law by teaching one of their father's slaves to read and write. Eventually, they left their home, family, and friends to become abolitionists.

Americans were very interested in what the Grimké sisters had to say because the sisters had grown up with slavery. Angelina Grimké became the first woman in the United States to stand up and speak in front of a lawmaking body. In 1838 she presented an antislavery petition signed by twenty thousand women to the Massachusetts state legislature.

## The Printer's Apprentice

WILLIAM LLOYD GARRISON was born in 1805 and grew up poor in Massachusetts. He worked for a printer when he was thirteen years old. After learning to be a printer, he became a journalist and a strong abolitionist.

When he was twenty-six years old, Garrison started a newspaper called *The Liberator*. He believed that slavery should immediately be abolished everywhere in the United States. Garrison was very critical of anyone who did not agree with his views. On one occasion, he burned a copy of the U.S. Constitution to show his anger at the government for continuing to allow slavery.

Garrison was against war, but he supported the Civil War. He was willing to do whatever was necessary to end slavery. He spoke, wrote, and published to support the abolitionist cause until 1865, when the United States officially ended slavery.

*William Lloyd Garrison,* right, *published an abolitionist newspaper. His opinions so angered his Boston neighbors that a mob once put a rope around his neck and led him around the streets of the city.*

*Northerners and Europeans admired Harriet Beecher Stowe,* above, *for writing* Uncle Tom's Cabin. *Southerners disliked her.*

## The Writer

HARRIET BEECHER STOWE wrote an important antislavery novel called *Uncle Tom's Cabin,* which was published in 1852. Born in 1811, Stowe lived for many years in Cincinnati, Ohio, a town just across the river from Kentucky, a slave state. While she lived there, she met escaped slaves and visited slaveholding communities. She based *Uncle Tom's Cabin* on what she saw and heard there.

Many people turned against slavery after reading Stowe's book. They were especially moved by Stowe's descriptions of slaves' families being separated by white slaveowners. In 1862 President Lincoln met Stowe. He reportedly said, "So you're the little woman who wrote the book that made this great war." *Uncle Tom's Cabin* was so popular that it was translated into at least twenty languages and performed as a play. More than two million copies were sold in the United States during the first ten years after it appeared.

# Time Line

1767: The Mason-Dixon Line, the boundary between Maryland (the South) and Pennsylvania (the North), is created.

1776: Representatives of the thirteen United States of America sign the Declaration of Independence.

1787: The Constitution of the United States is written.

1820: Congress passes the Missouri Compromise.

1848: The Mexican American War ends, and the United States wins a huge new territory that reaches to the Pacific coast.

1850: Congress decides how to handle slavery in the new territories won from Mexico. It also passes a tough new Fugitive Slave Law. These decisions make up the Compromise of 1850.

1854: The Kansas-Nebraska Act is passed.

1856: Kansas erupts in violence as slaveholders and abolitionists fight for control of the territory.

1857: The U.S. Supreme Court denies freedom to Dred Scott, a slave who had once lived on free soil.

1858: Abraham Lincoln and Stephen Douglas debate in the campaign for the U.S. Senate. Lincoln is defeated but becomes famous for his antislavery views.

October 1859: John Brown seizes the U.S. Armory at Harpers Ferry, Virginia. He is quickly captured, tried, convicted, and executed.

November 6, 1860: Abraham Lincoln is elected president of the United States.

December 20, 1860: South Carolina secedes from the United States.

January 1861: Mississippi, Florida, Alabama, Georgia, and Louisiana secede.

February 1, 1861: Texas secedes.

February 9, 1861: Jefferson Davis is elected president of the Confederate States of America.

April 12, 1861: The first shot of the Civil War is fired by Confederate forces on Fort Sumter in South Carolina.

April 15, 1861: Lincoln calls for 75,000 volunteers to fight the Confederates.

April 17, 1861: Virginia secedes.

May 1861: Arkansas, Tennessee, and North Carolina secede.

# Notes

**For quoted material in text:**

p. 8, David Donald, *Charles Sumner and the Coming of the Civil War* (New York: Alfred A. Knopf, 1960), 348.

p. 18, "John Quincy Adams: Slavery and the Constitution," In *Annals of America* (Chicago: Encyclopaedia Britannica, Inc., 1976), 4: 591.

p. 20, Allan Nevins, *Polk: The Diary of a President, 1845–1849* (New York: Longmans, Green and Co., 1929), 313.

p. 26, James M. McPherson, *Battle Cry of Freedom: The Civil War Era* (New York: Oxford University Press, 1988), 124.

p. 27, Roy P. Basler, *The Collected Works of Abraham Lincoln* (New Brunswick, NJ: Rutgers University Press, 1953), 4: 67.

p. 28, Ibid., 2: 266.

p. 30, *Congressional Globe*, 33d Cong., 1st sess., 25 May 1854, appendix, 769.

p. 30, James A. Rawley, *Race and Politics: "Bleeding Kansas" and the Coming of the Civil War* (Philadelphia: J. B. Lippincott Co., 1969), 81.

p. 30, McPherson, *Battle Cry of Freedom*, 146.

p. 30, Alice Nichols, *Bleeding Kansas* (New York: Oxford University Press, 1954), 29.

p. 33, William E. Gienapp, "The Crime against Sumner: The Caning of Charles Sumner and the Rise of the Republican Party," *Civil War History* (1979): 222.

p. 33, Stephen B. Oates, *To Purge This Land with Blood: A Biography of John Brown* (New York: Harper & Row, 1970), 129.

p. 33, Ibid., 133.

p. 33, Ibid.

p. 35, Basler, *The Collected Works of Abraham Lincoln*, 2: 461.

p. 37, Oates, *To Purge This Land with Blood*, 272.

p. 38, Shelby Foote, *The Civil War: A Narrative: Fort Sumter to Perryville* (New York: Random House, 1958), 31.

p. 38, Oates, *To Purge This Land with Blood*, 283.

p. 40, Thomas J. ("Stonewall") Jackson to Mary Anna Jackson, 2 December 1859, Documents, November 1859–January 1860, Archives, Virginia Military Institute, Lexington, VA.

p. 40, F. B. Sanborn, *The Life and Letters of John Brown* (Boston: Roberts Brothers, 1885), 620.

p. 43, Emerson D. Fite, *The Presidential Campaign of 1860* (New York: Macmillan Co., 1911), 243.

p. 43, Dwight Lowell Dumond, *Southern Editorials on Secession* (New York: Century Co., 1931), 223.

p. 43, William E. Baringer, *A House Dividing: Lincoln as President Elect* (Springfield, IL: Abraham Lincoln Association, 1945), 236.

p. 46, Dunbar Rowland, *Jefferson Davis: Constitutionalist: His Letters, Papers, and Speeches* (Jackson, MS: Mississippi Department of Archives and History, 1923), 5: 53.

p. 46, Emory M. Thomas, *The Confederate Nation, 1861–1865* (New York: Harper & Row, 1979), 307.

p. 46, Ibid., 320.

p. 47, Rowland, *Jefferson Davis*, 5: 53.

p. 47, Basler, *The Collected Works of Abraham Lincoln*, 4: 190.

p. 48, Ibid., 190.

p. 48, Foote, *The Civil War*, 35.

p. 49, Basler, *The Collected Works of Abraham Lincoln,* 4: 271.

p. 49  Ibid.

p. 49  Ibid.

p. 52, William Y. Thompson, *Robert Toombs of Georgia* (Baton Rouge: Louisiana State University Press, 1966), 168.

p. 56, Robert W. Johannsen, *Stephen A. Douglas* (New York: Oxford University Press, 1973), 868.

p. 57, Richard W. Johnson, *A Soldier's Reminisces in Peace and War* (Philadelphia: J. B. Lippincott, 1886), 156.

p. 58, *War of the Rebellion: Official Records of the Union and Confederate Armies,* series III, vol. 1 (Washington, D.C.: Government Printing Office, 1899), 99.

p. 58, Foote, *The Civil War,* 55.

p. 58, Rowland, *Jefferson Davis,* 5: 84.

p. 58, *War of the Rebellion,* 70.

p. 58, Ibid., 83.

p. 60, John G. Nicolay and John Hay, *Abraham Lincoln: A History* (New York: Century Co., 1890), 4: 152.

**For quoted material in sidebars:**

p. 12, George P. Rawick, *The American Slave: A Composite Autobiography* (Westport, CT: Greenwood Publishing Co., 1972), 6: 55.

p. 12, Ibid., 59.

p. 13, Ibid., 9.

p. 13, Ibid., 17.

p. 13, Ibid., 72.

p. 13, Ibid., 129, 130.

p. 16, "John Quincy Adams: Slavery and the Constitution," 4: 590.

p. 16  Ibid.

p. 16  Ibid.

p. 21, "Daniel Webster: Liberty and Union, Now and Forever, One and Inseparable," In *Annals of America* (Chicago: Encyclopaedia Britannica, Inc., 1976), 5: 355.

p. 65, McPherson, *Battle Cry of Freedom,* 90.

**For quoted material in captions:**

p. 33, Oates, *To Purge This Land with Blood,* 170, 171.

p. 46, Varina Davis, *Jefferson Davis: Ex-president of the Confederate States of America* (New York: Belford Co. Publishers, 1890), 2: 19.

p. 57, John Gibbon, *Personal Recollections of the Civil War* (Dayton, OH: Morningside Bookshop, 1978), 5.

p. 57  Ibid.

# Selected Bibliography

*Annals of America.* Vols. 4 and 5. Chicago: Encyclopaedia Britannica, Inc., 1976.

Basler, Roy P. *The Collected Works of Abraham Lincoln.* Vols. 2 and 4. New Brunswick, NJ: Rutgers University Press, 1953.

Boatner, Mark Mayo, III. *The Civil War Dictionary.* New York: David McKay Co., 1959.

Foote, Shelby. *The Civil War: A Narrative: Fort Sumter to Perryville.* New York: Random House, 1958.

Gibbon, John. *Personal Recollections of the Civil War.* Dayton, OH: Morningside Bookshop, 1978.

McPherson, James M. *Battle Cry of Freedom: The Civil War Era.* New York: Oxford University Press, 1988.

Nicolay, John G., and John Hay. *Abraham Lincoln: A History.* Vol. 4. New York: Century Co., 1890.

Oates, Stephen B. *To Purge This Land with Blood: A Biography of John Brown.* New York: Harper & Row, 1970.

Rawick, George P. *The American Slave: A Composite Autobiography.* Vol. 6. Westport, CT: Greenwood Publishing Co., 1972.

Rowland, Dunbar. *Jefferson Davis: Constitutionalist: His Letters, Papers, and Speeches.* Vol. 5. Jackson, MS: Mississippi Department of Archives and History, 1923.

*War of the Rebellion: Official Records of the Union and Confederate Armies.* Series III. Vol. 1. Washington, D.C.: Government Printing Office, 1899.

▻━◄◆▻━◯━◄◆▻━◄

# For More Information

**Books**

Burchard, Peter. *Lincoln and Slavery.* New York: Atheneum, 1999.

Ferris, Jeri. *Walking the Road to Freedom: A Story about Sojourner Truth.* Minneapolis: Carolrhoda Books, 1988.

Fleischner, Jennifer. *The Dred Scott Case: Testing the Right to Live Free.* Brookfield, CT: Millbrook Press, 1997.

Frazier, Joey. *Jefferson Davis.* New York: Chelsea House, 2000.

Freedman, Russell. *Lincoln: A Photobiography.* New York: Clarion Books, 1987.

Greene, Meg. *Slave Young, Slave Long: The American Slave Experience.* Minneapolis: Lerner Publications, 1999.

Hakim, Joy. *Liberty For All?* New York: Oxford University Press, 1994.

January, Brendan. *Fort Sumter.* New York: Children's Press, 1997.

———. *The Lincoln-Douglas Debates.* New York: Children's Press, 1998.

Kent, Zachary. *Jefferson Davis.* Chicago: Children's Press, 1993.

McPherson, Stephanie Sammartino. *Sisters against Slavery: A Story about Sarah and Angelina Grimké.* Minneapolis: Carolrhoda Books, 1999.

Smith, Carter, ed. *Prelude to War: A Sourcebook on the Civil War.* Brookfield, CT: Millbrook Press, 1993.

Toynton, Evelyn. *Growing Up in America, 1830–1860.* Brookfield, CT: Millbrook Press, 1995.

White, Deborah Gray. *Let My People Go: African Americans, 1804–1860.* New York: Oxford University Press, 1996.

### Videos

*Black Americans of Achievement Video Collection.* Bala Cynwyd, PA: Schlessinger Video Productions, 1992. Videocassettes. Includes information about Frederick Douglass, Sojourner Truth, and Harriet Tubman.

*The Civil War.* Walpole, NH: Florentine Films, 1990. Videocassette series. This PBS series by Ken Burns and narrated by David McCullough includes personal accounts and archival photos, as well as commentary by many writers on the period.

*Follow the Drinking Gourd: A Story of the Underground Railroad.*
Rowayton, CT: Rabbit Ears Productions, 1992. Videocassette. The story of one family's escape from slavery.

### Web Sites

<http://www.ajkids.com>
Users can ask questions about U.S. history in plain language and get connected to several different sites with answers.

<http://www.nationalgeographic.com/features/99/railroad/index.html>
Users take a journey as an escaped slave being led to freedom by Harriet Tubman on the Underground Railroad. Users can make choices along the way.

### Places to Visit

**Carter's Grove, Williamsburg, Virginia.** The mansion and slave quarters of a plantation that once encompassed 300,000 acres and 1,000 slaves.

**Fort Sumter National Monument, Charleston, South Carolina.** The restored site of the first clash of the Civil War.

**Harpers Ferry National Historical Park, Harpers Ferry, West Virginia.** Included in the site's more than two thousand acres is the arsenal where John Brown staged his 1859 raid.

**Lincoln Home National Historical Site, Springfield, Illinois.** The only home Lincoln ever owned, where he and his wife lived from 1844 to 1861. Lincoln's tomb can also be visited in Springfield.

**Lincoln Museum, Fort Wayne, Indiana.** Preserves the history and legacy of Lincoln through research, preservation of documents, exhibits, and continuing education.

# Index

# About the Authors

**James R. Arnold** was born in Illinois, and his family moved to Switzerland when he was a teenager. His fascination with the history of war was born on the battlefields of Europe. He returned to the United States for his college education. For the past twenty-five years, he and his wife, Roberta Wiener, have lived and farmed in the Shenandoah Valley of Virginia and toured all the Civil War battlefields.

Mr. Arnold's great-great-grandfather was shot and killed in Fairfax, Virginia, because he voted against secession. Another ancestor served in an Ohio regiment during the Civil War. Mr. Arnold has written more than twenty books about American and European wars, and he has contributed to many others.

**Roberta Wiener** grew up in Pennsylvania and completed her education in Washington, D.C. After many years of touring battlefields and researching books with her husband, James R. Arnold, she has said, "The more I learn about war, the more fascinating it becomes." Ms. Wiener has coauthored nine books with Mr. Arnold and edited numerous educational books, including a children's encyclopedia. She has also worked as an archivist for the U.S. Army.

>-+-•>-•-O-<•-+-•<

# Picture Acknowledgments

Architect of the Capitol: 51T. *Frank Leslie's Illustrated Newspaper*: 58, 60. Harpers Ferry National Park: 38. *Harpers Weekly*: 11T, 38-39, 30, 31, 42, 44B. Kansas State Historical Society: 30-31. Library of Congress: front cover, back cover, 6-7, 8T, 9T, 12, 13, 14-15, 18, 19, 23, 24, 27, 28, 34, 44T, 46, 47, 48, 50-51, 54-55, 56-57, 59, 61, 63T. The Lincoln Museum, Fort Wayne, Indiana: 35, 43. Maryland Historical Society: 8-9. National Archives: 16, 20, 21, 25, 29, 32, 33, 45, 57T, 63B, 64, 65. National Park Service: 52. U.S. Army Military Institute: 10. Virginia Military Institute: 36-37. West Point Museum Collection, U.S. Military Academy: 50T.

Maps by Jerry Malone and Tim Kissel.